THE HISTORY OF THE NEW YORK JETS

Published by Creative Education
123 South Broad Street
Mankato, Minnesota 56001
Creative Education is an imprint of The Creative Company.

DESIGN AND PRODUCTION BY **EVANSDAY DESIGN**

LIBRARY OF CONGRESS CATALOGING-IN-PUBLICATION DATA

Goodman, Michael E.
The history of the New York Jets / by Michael E. Goodman.
p. cm. — (NFL today)
Summary: Traces the history of the team from its beginnings through 2003.
ISBN 1-58341-307-3
1. New York Jets (Football team)—History—Juvenile literature. [1. New York Jets
(Football team)—History. 2. Football—History.] I. Title. II. Series.

GV956.N42G64 2004
796.332'64'097471—dc22   2003062576

First edition

9 8 7 6 5 4 3 2 1

COVER PHOTO: quarterback Chad Pennington

PHOTOGRAPHS BY
AP/Wide World Photos, Corbis (Bettmann, Reuters), Getty Images, Icon Sports Media Inc., SportsChrome USA

Michael E. Goodman

NEW YORK CITY MAY BE LOCATED ON THE EAST COAST OF THE UNITED STATES, BUT IT IS THE CENTER OF THE COUNTRY'S BUSINESS, CULTURAL, AND MEDIA INDUSTRIES. ORIGINATING FROM A SMALL DUTCH SETTLEMENT IN THE 1640S, NEW YORK HAS GROWN INTO AMERICA'S BIGGEST CITY—A MEGALOPOLIS THAT SPREADS OVER PARTS OF THE STATES OF NEW YORK, NEW JERSEY, AND CONNECTICUT. FOR DECADES, NEW YORK CITY HAS BEEN REPRESENTED BY TWO NATIONAL FOOTBALL LEAGUE (NFL) TEAMS: THE GIANTS OF THE NATIONAL CONFERENCE AND THE JETS OF THE AMERICAN CONFERENCE. IN CONTRAST TO THE OLDER GIANTS FRANCHISE, WHICH WAS KNOWN FOR ITS CONSERVATIVE PLAYING STYLE, THE JETS FRANCHISE—WHICH WAS BORN IN 1960 AS THE TITANS (ANOTHER WORD FOR GIANTS)—QUICKLY LIVED UP TO ITS NAME WITH AN EXCITING, HIGH-FLYING STYLE.

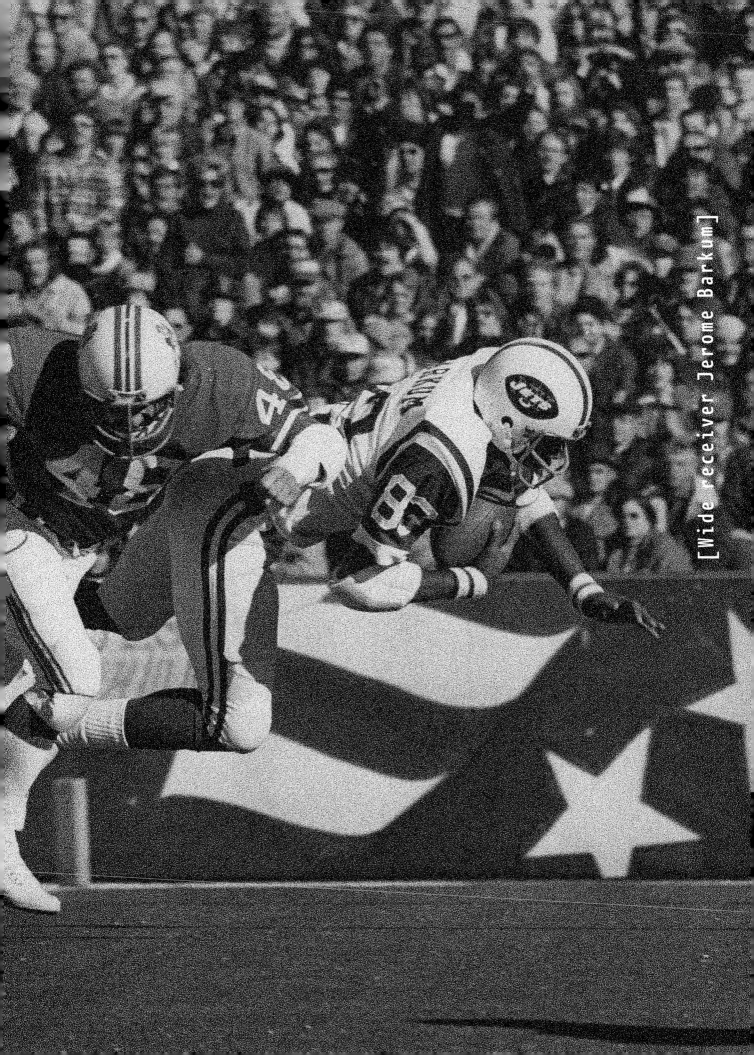

[Wide receiver Jerome Barkum]

THE TITANS BEGAN playing in 1960 as part of the American Football League (AFL), a new league formed to rival the NFL. The Titans' owner was former broadcaster Harry Wismer, who immediately challenged the city's NFL team by proclaiming, "We're called Titans because titans are bigger than giants."

The new club posted a respectable 7–7 record its first year thanks to a potent offense that revolved around the passing of quarterback Al Dorow and the receiving of ends Art Powell and Don Maynard. Maynard became the team's first star. With his great hands and elusive moves, he scored 88 touchdowns during his career (still a club record) and eventually earned a place in the Pro Football Hall of Fame.

Don Maynard was the first player signed by the Titans and immediately became one of the AFL's top stars^

Weeb Ewbank spent 11 seasons as New York's head coach and was later inducted into the Hall of Fame ^

Despite Maynard's efforts, the Titans were not big winners on the field or financially. By the middle of the 1962 season, Wismer was nearly broke and was forced to give up the team. A group led by former television executive David (Sonny) Werblin then purchased the club for $1 million.

Werblin gave the team a complete makeover. He changed its name from Titans to Jets and replaced the players' drab blue and gold uniforms with much brighter kelly green and white ones. Then he brought in veteran coach Weeb Ewbank to reshape the club on the field. Ewbank had previously coached the Baltimore Colts to NFL championships in 1958 and 1959. He was a calm leader who spoke patiently with players rather than trying to fire them up with yelling. "Weeb Ewbank treated us like men, and I appreciate that," recalled former Jets center John Schmitt.

Coach Ewbank's Jets didn't have a great record in 1963 (5-8-1), but they started receiving more fan support in New York. The fans cheered even louder the next year when the Jets drafted All-American fullback Matt Snell out of Ohio State University. Snell finished the 1964 season as the league's second-leading rusher and was named AFL Rookie of the Year.

Excitement was building in Shea Stadium, the Jets' new home. It reached a fever pitch in 1965 with the arrival of flashy quarterback Joe Willie Namath. Werblin had convinced Namath to join the AFL instead of the NFL by offering him a three-year contract for the amazing sum of $427,000. Overnight, Namath became the highest-paid American athlete in any sport. With his good looks and cocky attitude, Namath became a star both on the field and off, and sportswriters nicknamed him "Broadway Joe."

Broadway Joe quickly proved that he was worth his big contract. In 1966, he led the Jets to a 6–6–2 record by throwing long bombs to receivers Don Maynard and George Sauer Jr. Everything was looking bright for the Jets until Namath began struggling with knee problems.

Namath played through the pain the next year, leading the Jets to their first winning record (8–5–1) and becoming the first pro quarterback in either the AFL or NFL to pass for more than 4,000 yards in a season. Other Jets players also had great years in 1967. Sauer led the AFL with 75 receptions, Maynard topped the league with 1,434 receiving yards, and rookie running back Emerson Boozer paired with Snell to give New York the AFL's best rushing duo. The Jets were ready to soar.

Every Jets home game in 1967 was sold out as fans packed in to see such stars as halfback Emerson Boozer^

x

Down! Green 11 Set! Hut!

JOE WILLIE'S GUARANTEE>

JETS FANS HAD high expectations in 1968. The club

had the league's top quarterback directing the AFL's best

offense, as well as a great defense led by end Gerry

Philbin, linebacker Al Atkinson, and cornerback Johnny

Sample. The Jets rolled over opponents, finishing with

an 11–3 record and earning a berth in the AFL champi-

onship game against the Oakland Raiders.

In a tight battle at Shea Stadium, New York edged out

Oakland 27–23 thanks to three Namath touchdown passes

and two field goals by kicker Jim Turner. The next stop

on the "Jets Express" was Miami, where the Jets faced

the NFL champion Baltimore Colts in Super Bowl III.

One of the most famous players of all time, Joe Namath carried the Jets to the 1968 Super Bowl

Speedy receiver Wesley Walker was part of the Jets' 1970s rebuilding effort after their world championship

That Super Bowl was a turning point in professional football history. It was more than just a game between two teams—it was also a war between two leagues. The Jets were made 18-point underdogs, and some writers predicted that the powerful Colts would win by 30 points. Joe Namath had other ideas. "Our team is better than any NFL team," he announced boldly. "We're going to win Sunday. In fact, I guarantee it."

Namath and his teammates backed up the guarantee. Millions of football fans watched in disbelief as New York dominated the game. The Jets scored first on a Snell touchdown run, and their defense refused to budge all game long. The 16–7 Jets win was one of the most shocking upsets in sports history. It also helped pave the way for a successful merger between the two leagues before the 1970 season.

After the Super Bowl win, Jets fans began to talk about a dynasty. They were confident that Namath's arm could carry them to more titles. Unfortunately, Namath's battered knees and nagging injuries to other team leaders quickly grounded the Jets.

AFTER JOINING THE NFL in 1970, the Jets settled near the middle of the American Football Conference (AFC) standings. Namath was still a fine passer, and receiver Jerome Barkum and flamboyant running back John Riggins added power to the offense. However, the club's record continued to decline.

When the Jets won a total of only six games in 1975 and 1976, the team's owners started making changes. First a new coach—former Jets linebacker Walt Michaels—was brought in. Then Michaels turned the offense over to young quarterback Richard Todd and released Namath. Jets fans bid a sad farewell to Broadway Joe, who ended his New York career with more than 27,000 passing yards and 170 touchdowns—both still club records.

The first 1,000-yard rusher in club history, John Riggins was known for his sledgehammer running style^

Fiery defensive end Mark Gastineau set team records for sacks in a season (22) and career sacks (107.5)^

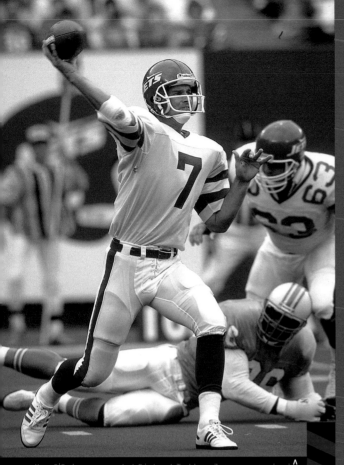

Ken O'Brien succeeded Richard Todd as Jets quarterback ^

Coach Michaels's Jets, featuring Todd and defensive linemen Joe Klecko and Mark Gastineau, began revving up crowds at Shea Stadium. The hard-rushing Klecko and Gastineau formed the "New York Sack Exchange," and Gastineau often celebrated his sacks by doing a dance over the fallen quarterback. The owners of other NFL teams didn't enjoy the dance, however, and soon passed the "Gastineau Rule" to outlaw showy celebrations after a sack.

In 1981, the Jets reached the NFL playoffs for the first time. Against the Buffalo Bills in the opening round, the Jets fell behind 24–0 and then made a remarkable comeback before losing 31–27. Coach Michaels wasn't discouraged, however. "If all of New York hasn't fallen in love with this team yet," he said, "then they will in 1982."

The 1982 Jets advanced all the way to the AFC championship game, where they lost to the Miami Dolphins 14–0. Michaels resigned after the loss and was replaced by new coach Joe Walton. That was only one major change for the Jets. The club also moved its home base across the Hudson River to Giants Stadium before the 1983 season. Jets fans found their way to New Jersey and filled the larger stadium with even louder shouts of "J–E–T–S! Jets! Jets! Jets!"

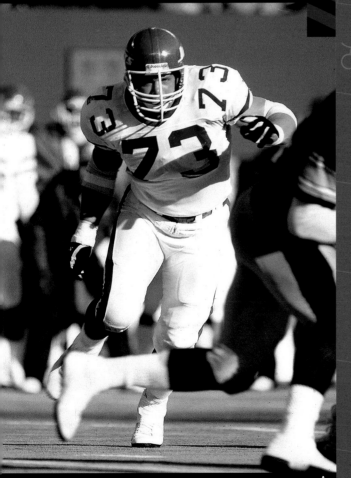

Star pass rusher Joe Klecko spent 11 years in New York ^

The loudest cheers were for quarterback Ken O'Brien, halfback Freeman McNeil, and wide receiver Al Toon, who led the club to the playoffs in both 1985 and 1986. Then the cheers turned to jeers as the team plummeted in the standings near the end of the decade. After a miserable 4–12 season in 1989, Walton was fired, and a new rebuilding process began.

THE JETS FINALLY made it back to the playoffs in 1991, thanks in large part to the efforts of record-setting place-kicker Pat Leahy. Then the club took another nosedive in the two seasons that followed, and even the arrival of veteran quarterback Boomer Esiason could not turn the team's fortunes around. After another losing campaign in 1994, team owner Leon Hess announced, "I'm 80 years old, and I want results now. I'm entitled to some enjoyment from this team, and that means winning."

Hess had to suffer through two more losing seasons, however, before the Jets finally found a winning combination under new head coach Bill Parcells. Parcells knew all about winning in Giants Stadium, having previously led the Giants to two Super Bowl victories. Then he had turned a broken-down New England Patriots team into a Super Bowl contender.

Parcells's Jets lineup featured two key offensive weapons: receivers Wayne Chrebet and Keyshawn Johnson. The two were as different as night and day. The 5-foot-9 Chrebet was quiet, steady, and tough—more of a hard worker than a natural athlete. The 6-foot-3 Johnson was taller and smoother than Chrebet. He was also talkative and flashy. Together, they formed a potent receiving duo.

Under Coach Parcells's magic touch, the Jets jumped from a 1–15 record in 1996 to 9–7 in 1997. The coach then promised his players that more and better changes were ahead. "I told them that nobody could stand still," he later recalled. "You either get better, or you get worse. It's that simple."

To make the team better, Parcells signed three free agents—running back Curtis Martin, center Kevin Mawae, and quarterback Vinny Testaverde. The new arrivals helped turn the Jets into an offensive powerhouse in 1998 and led the club to its first division title since its AFL days in 1969. Testaverde set a team record with 29 touchdown passes; Chrebet and Johnson each posted more than 1,000 receiving yards, and Martin recorded his fourth straight season with more than 1,000 rushing yards.

In the playoffs, the Jets defeated the Jacksonville Jaguars 34–24 to reach the AFC championship game against the Denver Broncos, the defending Super Bowl champs. But in the title contest, Denver capitalized on six New York turnovers to crush the Jets' Super Bowl dreams, 23–10.

Short but fierce receiver Wayne Chrebet earned a reputation as a clutch performer in the late 1990s^

PINNING HOPES ON PENNINGTON>

PARCELLS STEPPED DOWN after the 1999 season

and handed the coaching reins to his former assistant,

Al Groh. Groh led the Jets for only one year, but he made

a key move that would brighten the club's future, select-

Under Pennington, the Jets rebounded from a disappointing 2–5 start to finish the year as AFC Eastern Division champs with a 9–7 record. The young quarterback also led the NFL in passer rating, a measure of passing accuracy and performance. Pennington's poise under fire impressed fans, coaches, and teammates. "Chad is like a coach on the field," said Jets tight end Anthony Becht. "He understands everything. He knows what has to be done in every situation."

Pennington was only one young star that Jets fans were counting on to keep the team near the top of the AFC. Running back LaMont Jordan appeared ready to succeed Curtis Martin as a star rusher, and speedy wide receiver Santana Moss was set to turn Pennington's long bombs into touchdowns. On defense, end John Abraham and huge tackle Dewayne Robertson were expected to drive opposing quarterbacks crazy in 2004 and beyond.

The history of the New York Jets includes the highest highs and lowest lows, but today's team seems to have at last reached cruising altitude near the top of the AFC. After celebrating one Super Bowl victory and then enduring many forgettable seasons, Jets fans throughout the New York metropolitan area are looking forward to the day when green and white are the colors of an NFL champion once more.

Like early star Don Maynard, Santana Moss scared opponents with his speed and unpredictable moves^

INDEX>

A

Abraham, John 30
AFC championship games 19, 26
AFL championship 12
AFL championship game 12
AFL seasons 6, 9, 10, 12, 15
Atkinson, Al 12

B

Barkum, Jerome 5, 16
Becht, Anthony 30
Boozer, Emerson 10, 10–11

C

Chrebet, Wayne 24, 26–27

D

division championships 24, 30
Dorow, Al 6

E

Edwards, Herman 28
Esiason, Boomer 22, 23
Ewbank, Weeb 8–9, 9

G

Gastineau, Mark 18, 19
Giants Stadium 19, 22
Groh, Al 28

H

Hall of Fame 6
Hess, Leon 22

J

Johnson, Keyshawn 24
Jordan, LaMont 30

K

Klecko, Joe 19, 19

L

Leahy, Pat 22

M

Martin, Curtis 24, 24–25, 30
Mawae, Kevin 24
Maynard, Don 6, 7, 9, 10
McNeil, Freeman 21
Michaels, Walt 16, 19
Moss, Santana 30, 30–31

N

Namath, Joe 10, 12, 13, 15, 16
New York Titans 4, 6, 9

O

O'Brien, Ken 19, 21

P

Parcells, Bill 22, 24, 28
Pennington, Chad 28, 29, 30
Philbin, Gerry 12
Powell, Art 6

R

Riggins, John 16, 17
Robertson, Dewayne 30

S

Sample, Johnny 12
Sauer, George Jr. 10
Schmitt, John 9
Shea Stadium 10, 12, 19
Snell, Matt 9, 10, 15
Super Bowl 12, 15, 30

T

team records 6, 16, 24
Testaverde, Vinny 24
Todd, Richard 16, 19
Toon, Al 20–21, 21
Turner, Jim 12

W

Walker, Wesley 14–15
Walton, Joe 19, 21
Werblin, David (Sonny) 9, 10
Wismer, Harry 6, 9